BUILDING BLOCKS OF MATTER

ELEMENTS AND COMPOUNDS

Louise and Richard Spilsbury

Heinemann Library
Chicago, Illinois

Customer Service 888-454-2279
Visit our website at www.heinemannraintree.com

Designed by Richard Parker and Tinstar Design Ltd, www.tinstar.co.uk
Printed and bound in China by Leo Paper Group

11 10 09 08 07
10 9 8 7 6 5 4 3 2 1

Library of Congress Cataloging-in-Publication Data
Spilsbury, Louise.
 Elements and compounds / Louise and Richard Spilsbury.
    p. cm. -- (Building blocks of matter)
 Includes bibliographical references and index.
 ISBN-13: 978-1-4034-9338-5 (lib. bdg.)
 ISBN-10: 1-4034-9338-3 (lib. bdg.)
 ISBN-13: 978-1-4034-9343-9 (pbk.)
 ISBN-10: 1-4034-9343-X (pbk.)
 1. Chemical elements--Juvenile literature. I. Spilsbury, Richard, 1963-
 II. Title.
 QD466.S65 2007
 546--dc22
                    2006025743

Acknowledgments
The publishers would like to thank the following for permission to reproduce photographs: Alamy pp. 4 (Elmtree Images), 5 (GC Minerals), 25 (Marco Solis), 16 (Maximilian Weinzierl); Corbis pp. 13 (Alan Schein Photography), 15 (David Butow; SABA), 26 (Onne van der Wal), 21 (photocuisine), 10, 11, 20 (Royalty Free); Getty Images pp. 6 (Photodisc), 8 (Photographer's Choice/Brian Stablyk); Harcourt Education pp. 22 (Devon Shaw), 17 top & bottom (Trevor Clifford), 27 top & bottom (Tudor Photography); Photodisc pp. 5, 18; Photos.com p. 24; Science Photo Library pp. 7 (CERN), 9 (Charles D. Winters), 23 (Cordelia Molloy), 12 (R. Maisonneuve, Publiphoto Diffusion).

Cover photograph of a close-up of various-sized water droplets on a pane of glass reproduced with permission of Science Photo Library (Bill Longcore).

Every effort has been made to contact copyright holders of any material reproduced in this book. Any omissions will be rectified in subsequent printings if notice is given to the publishers.

The publishers would like to thank Nick Sample for his help in the preparation of this book.

Contents

Any words appearing in the text in bold, **like this**, are explained in the Glossary.

What Are Elements?

What do wolves, mountains, computers, and yachts have in common? They are all made up of different **elements**, like anything else in the universe. Elements are substances that contain only one type of **atom**. Three elements you may have heard of are aluminum, iron, and carbon. Steel contains both iron and carbon atoms, so it is not an element.

Elements and their atoms

Aluminum cans, like the ones you buy soda in, are made of just one element. If we cut a can into smaller and smaller pieces, we would finally end up with atoms of aluminum. These are the smallest pieces possible of the element aluminum. Atoms are far too small for us to see. If an atom were the size of an apple, an apple would be as big as Earth!

A drink can made of aluminum contains billions and billions of aluminum atoms.

Naming elements

Each different element has its own name. However, names differ depending on the language people speak. For example, iron is *hierro* in Spanish and *loha* in Hindi. People can avoid confusion by using internationally agreed upon names for elements.

An element's international name is a **chemical symbol**, usually made up of the first letters of their English name. For example, the symbol for carbon is C and the symbol for cobalt is Co. Other elements have symbols based on names in different languages. For example, the symbol for iron is Fe, from its Latin name, *ferrum*.

Did you know?
Early elements

Everything that has weight and takes up space is called matter. Over 2,500 years ago, many people believed all matter was made up of four elements. These were fire, air, water, and earth, which included all living and nonliving matter. These beliefs changed around 350 years ago, when a scientist named Robert Boyle said matter contains many different elements made of different atoms.

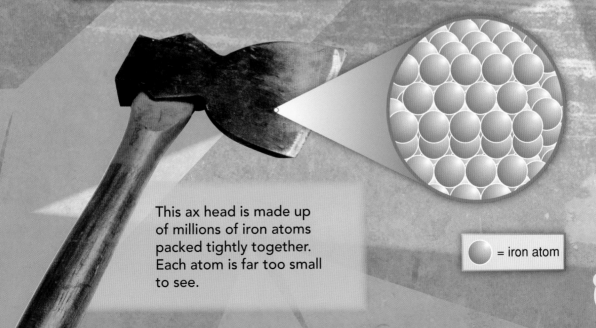

This ax head is made up of millions of iron atoms packed tightly together. Each atom is far too small to see.

= iron atom

How many different elements are there?

There are about 115 different elements, and 90 of these make up most things on Earth. Some elements, such as gold and copper, can be found naturally as lumps on the ground, in rivers, or in rocks. These were identified before people knew that they were different elements. Other elements have been discovered by scientists in experiments—for example, on different types of rocks or soils.

The other 25 elements are not found naturally. Scientists have made these other elements by using special equipment. An example of these unusual elements is Einsteinium, named after the famous scientist Albert Einstein. Some new elements are so rare they have only ever been spotted once!

All planets, not just Earth, are made of elements. Iron on Mars gives it a red color.

CASE STUDY:
Making a new element

In 2004 scientists made a new element called ununpentium. They did this by making atoms of calcium smash very fast into atoms of an element called americium. In equipment called **particle** accelerators, atoms can move almost at the speed of light. A particle accelerator is a very long straight or circular tube, sometimes several miles long.

In this experiment, calcium atoms were released at one end. They moved faster and faster through the tube. Once they were moving fast enough, the calcium atoms smashed into the americium atoms. Enormous detectors around the americium measured the size, speed, and direction of fragments of atoms produced by the collision. They detected that four new atoms of ununpentium had been created. A fraction of a second later, they had turned into other elements.

This is a particle accelerator used to create new elements.

How Are Elements Grouped?

People group **elements** together based on their properties. The **physical properties** of an element are things we can measure or observe without changing it into a different substance. For example, hardness, color, and smell are all physical properties. The **chemical properties** of an element are how it behaves when it is put together with other elements. For example, iron **atoms** combine with oxygen atoms to make **rust**, but gold atoms do not. We cannot tell a substance's chemical properties by looking at or touching it.

States

Any element is naturally found in one of three **states** of matter: **solid**, **liquid**, or **gas**. This is one of its physical properties. Atoms in gases such as oxygen move quickly. They are further apart than in liquids such as iodine, where the atoms flow over each other. Atoms in solids, such as copper, are the slowest moving of any state. They are packed closely together.

One physical property of helium is that it is lighter than air. We use it to make balloons float.

Arranging elements

Scientists arrange all the 115 elements in a chart called the **periodic table** (see page 28). The elements are grouped together according to their physical and chemical properties. For example, gases similar to helium are put near each other in the table in one column. Although each element has different properties, there are three general groups of elements, called **metals**, **nonmetals**, and **semimetals**.

Did you know?
Changing state

Any element can change physical properties by changing state. Elements usually change state when they are heated or cooled. The element mercury is a metal that is liquid at room temperature. Some thermometers show temperature by how high or low mercury has flowed inside thin glass tubes. However, mercury thermometers cannot be used in Antarctica because the mercury freezes into a solid at the low temperatures there.

This is mercury. One old name for this element is quicksilver, because it looks like **melted** silver.

What Are Metals?

About three-quarters of all **elements** are **metals**. Metals are grouped together because they have broadly similar **physical properties**. Metals are generally strong, shiny, heavy, and hard **solids**. However, metals can look very different. For instance, mercury is a shiny **liquid** metal. However, potassium is white, dull, and so soft it can be cut with a knife. Metals are used for different purposes, depending on their properties.

Shiny surfaces

Some metal elements, such as silver, gold, and platinum, are used to make jewelry and other precious items. Metals usually reflect light very well so they look shiny. These precious metals do not easily combine or **react** with other elements, so they always look good. Other metals, such as iron, lead, and copper, react with air or water. This forms different substances on their surface, making them get duller or change color.

Precious metals are valuable because they stay shiny, and also because they are rare.

Hard and strong

Metals get their hardness and strength from the strong links or **bonds** between their **atoms**. Inside any atom there are small, fast-moving **particles** called **electrons**. Some of the electrons in metals are shared between atoms and help pull the atoms firmly together.

Iron is the most common hard metal. It is used to make things ranging from railroads and bridges to cars and ships.

Metal is used to make tough frameworks for the world's tallest buildings.

Did you know?
Plumbum

The **chemical symbol** for the element lead is Pb, which is short for *plumbum*. This is the ancient Latin name for lead used by the Romans. Lead is a very soft metal that is easy to bend and mold into shape. The Romans used it to make pipes to take water to and from public baths and houses. Today, the word "plumbing" still means piping for water.

Stretching and flattening

Many metals can be stretched into thin wires or flattened into sheets. Other elements, such as carbon, would break or snap. Softer metals such as copper are more easily stretched or flattened than harder metals such as iron. People heat metals to make them softer before using hammers or powerful rolling machines to flatten them. Strong grips can pull them into wires.

Passing on electricity

Electricity is a force created by moving electrons. Most metals are good at passing on, or **conducting**, electricity. This is because the electrons shared by metal atoms can move around easily within metals. Metals such as silver and gold are the best **conductors**, but they are expensive to use. They are used only in small amounts within electrical machines such as computers.

Each of these thin copper wires conducts electricity. The metal is covered by colored plastic to stop electricity from passing between wires.

Did you know?
Magnetic elements

Magnetism is a type of force that makes atoms pull closer together or push further apart than usual. It is caused by spinning electrons. In a few metal elements, this force is strong. The most common magnetic elements are iron, nickel, and cobalt. In other elements, including most metals, the magnetism is so weak that they are called nonmagnetic.

Heat conduction

Most metals are good at conducting heat. Heat is a form of energy. Things feel hot when atoms inside them are vibrating fast. They feel cold when atoms are moving slowly. When the shared electrons in metals crash into faster-vibrating atoms, they move even faster. These quick electrons travel to the cold end of the metal. There, they knock into cold atoms and make them vibrate faster.

Some metals are better heat conductors than others. For example, copper warms up thirty times faster than stainless steel.

Cooking pans are usually made of iron. Iron conducts heat well and **melts** only at temperatures far greater than those used on stoves or in ovens.

13

CASE STUDY:
Mining platinum

Platinum is a rare and precious metal. It is hard and melts at high temperatures. It does not easily combine with other elements, but it helps different elements react together more easily. Platinum is found in rocks in countries such as South Africa. It is usually found mixed with similar metals called platinum group metals or PGM. Rocks containing useful metals are called **ores**.

Miners use explosives to get PGM ore from within other rocks. They grind the ore up into powder and heat it up to over 2,190 °F (1,200 °C) to melt the metals. Magnets and chemicals are used to remove other metals, leaving just platinum. It takes over 10 tons of ore to produce only 1 ounce (30 grams) of pure platinum—the weight of a small hen's egg.

These are chunks of platinum and other metals in PGM ore.

What Are Nonmetals?

Nonmetals are **elements** with properties that are different than those of **metals**. For example, nonmetals are not shiny. They cannot **conduct** heat or **electricity** well. If **solid**, they **melt** at low temperatures.

Types of nonmetals

Over half of all nonmetal elements are naturally found as **gases** in air. The most common are nitrogen and oxygen. Most of the other nonmetals, including sulfur and carbon, are solid. These elements are generally brittle, which means they crumble or break when stretched or flattened. Bromine is the only nonmetal found as a **liquid**.

How we use gas elements

Gas elements have different **chemical properties** that we use for different purposes. Oxygen **reacts** easily with materials such as coal or wood. The reaction releases heat, which is called burning. Other gases such as argon do not burn. Argon is put around the hot, glowing wires in some lightbulbs. This stops them from burning up, so they last longer.

Neon gas glows red when electricity is passed through it. It is used for bright signs like this.

15

Using other nonmetal elements

The element carbon is found as very different types of matter. One is graphite, which is fairly soft and used to make pencil leads. The other is diamond. Diamond crystals are very precious. They are the hardest known material. They are used on drill bits and saws used to cut hard materials such as metals.

Thin layers of carbon atoms are weakly joined together in graphite. Pencils can draw or write because carbon atoms rub off, leaving a mark on paper.

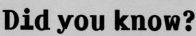

Did you know?
Same element, different types

Graphite and diamond are both pure carbon. They are not two different **states**, like water and ice. They have different **physical properties** because of the **bonds** between the carbon **atoms**. There are more bonds between carbon atoms in diamond than in graphite. (See the "carbon challenge" demonstration on the next page.)

Demonstration
Carbon challenge

Here is a demonstration of the different physical properties of graphite and diamond using small balls of modeling clay and a box of plastic toothpicks. The balls represent carbon atoms and the toothpicks are bonds between them.

You will need:
- some modeling clay
- a box of plastic toothpicks

Graphite
In graphite, each carbon atom is attached to three others.

Procedure:
1. Take ten balls of clay and join them into two six-sided hexagons using toothpicks. Be careful not to prick your fingers!
2. Make two more hexagons and fix them on top of the first. See how easy it is to slide the top layer off the bottom one. This atom arrangement makes graphite soft.

Diamond
In diamond, each carbon atom is bonded strongly to four others.

Procedure:
1. Take a ball and put four toothpicks in it.
2. Complete a model with more balls and toothpicks like the one on the right. It is difficult to move each ball because each is held firmly in place by the toothpicks around it. This is why diamond is so hard.

Unusual elements

Some elements have properties in between metals and nonmetals. They are often called **semimetals**. The best-known example of a semimetal is silicon. Silicon is gray and shiny, like many metals. However, silicon is unlike metals because it does not conduct electricity well and it breaks when stretched or flattened.

Silicon can be made to conduct electricity better wherever its surface is painted with special chemicals. Machines are used to paint detailed electrical circuits on small, flat crystals of silicon called silicon chips. Silicon chips control complicated equipment such as computers and cell phones.

This portable computer, or laptop, is controlled by a silicon chip the size of a large postage stamp.

Did you know?
Common as silicon

Silicon is a very common element on our planet. It makes up about a quarter of Earth's weight. It is sometimes found as pure silicon crystals, but more often it combines with oxygen to form silica. Sand, quartz, and clay are made of silica combined with other elements.

What Are Compounds?

Atoms are not always found on their own. A **molecule** is a group of two or more atoms **bonded** together. Sometimes atoms of the same **element** join up. Other times, atoms of two or more different elements join together. This type of molecule is called a **compound**.

Each compound has a particular combination of elements. For example, each molecule of carbon dioxide is made of one carbon atom and two oxygen atoms. Some compounds are more complicated. For example, a sulfuric acid molecule contains two hydrogen, one sulfur, and four oxygen atoms.

Naming compounds

Compounds are named by grouping together **chemical symbols** and the names of the elements they contain. Little numbers are added next to the symbols to show how many of each atom there are. For example, carbon dioxide is CO_2 and sulfuric acid is H_2SO_4.

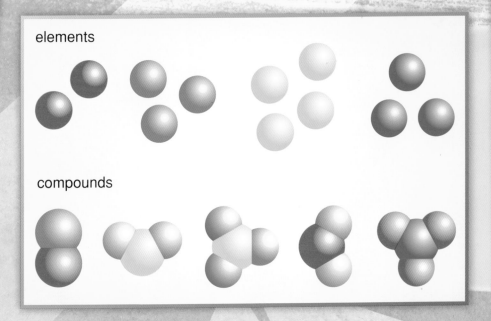

elements

compounds

Some compounds are made from just two different elements. Others are made up of many different types of element.

How do compounds form?

Elements join together into compounds during **chemical reactions**. During a chemical reaction, bonds form between different elements. **Electrons** on the outside of the different atoms are shared or exchanged between the atoms. This produces a pulling force between the atoms.

Some reactions happen naturally. Iron **rusts** in air because iron atoms **react** with oxygen atoms to make the reddish compound iron oxide (rust). Other reactions need some help. For example, we must heat wood so that it reacts with oxygen and starts to burn.

Did you know?
Weak rust

Rust has different physical properties than iron. Rust is crumbly and weak, while iron is hard and solid. Iron objects left outside for a long time, such as bikes, cars, or boats, may become unsafe to use if they get too rusty. Rust forms quickest in wet, salty conditions, such as in seawater. This is because atoms in water and salt help oxygen react faster with iron.

Rust makes tough objects such as this car crumble into useless scrap.

Properties of compounds

Each element has its own **physical properties** and **chemical properties**, but a compound has different properties than the elements it contains. For example, sodium is a soft **metal** element that burns and reacts dangerously with water. Chlorine is a poisonous, greenish, **nonmetal gas**. The compound that forms from sodium and chlorine is sodium chloride. Its common name is salt. Salt has different physical properties than chlorine and sodium. It is a **solid** made up of small, soft, white crystals. It also has different chemical properties. Salt does not react when left in air or put in water.

Permanent change

If you **melt** ice into water, you can then freeze the water to make ice again. Changing an element's physical **state** like this is a **reversible** change. However, most chemical reactions are not reversible. Once sodium and chlorine combine, you cannot separate them again.

The compound salt (sodium chloride) is safe to eat in small quantities on food, but the elements sodium and chlorine are dangerous on their own.

Which Natural Compounds Are Most Important?

Many important **compounds** are found naturally on Earth. Rocks and wood are two examples. A few, including water, carbon dioxide, and other carbon compounds, are essential to all life on Earth.

Water

Water is a compound of hydrogen and oxygen. It is found on Earth as a **solid**, **liquid**, and **gas**. Ice is solid water that is found naturally in cold places, such as the poles. Water in the gas **state** is called water vapor.

The **physical properties** of water are that it is a colorless, tasteless liquid that is good at **dissolving** many compounds, including salt and sugar. The salt or sugar **molecules** separate from each other in water and become surrounded by water molecules. Water is a poor heat **conductor**. However, it **conducts electricity** well. That is why it is dangerous to use electrical equipment near water.

This waterfall is part of the water cycle, which moves Earth's water around the planet.

Did you know?

Dinosaur drinks

Water formed billions of years ago from gases in space. It collected inside tiny lumps of clay and ice floating in space. These bits joined together to form our planet. Throughout history, the water has formed oceans and areas of ice in different places at different times. However, the total amount of water on Earth has always remained the same. Just imagine—you could be drinking the same molecules of water that dinosaurs drank!

Carbon dioxide

Carbon is a solid **element** rarely found on its own. It **reacts** easily with other elements, so it is usually found in compounds. Carbon dioxide is a compound formed when oxygen reacts with carbon. It is naturally found as a gas in the air and its main **chemical property** is that it does not burn or react with many substances. People use carbon dioxide in fire extinguishers to put out electrical fires.

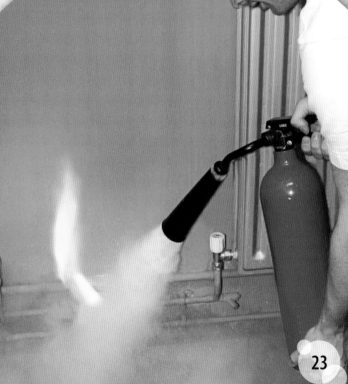

Carbon dioxide stops fires by preventing oxygen from reacting with other elements or compounds to release heat.

23

Food and oxygen

Most food is made up of carbon compounds. Some of these come from plants and others come from animals that eat plants.

Plants use the energy from sunlight to create a carbon compound called glucose. It is made from carbon dioxide in the air and water. The **chemical reaction** that forms it is called photosynthesis. Photosynthesis also produces oxygen, which most animals need to breathe.

When animals feed on plants or each other, some glucose breaks down inside their bodies. This releases energy, which animals use to live, move, and grow. It also releases carbon dioxide into the air.

Fossil fuels

Oil, coal, and gas are all carbon compounds. They formed from remains of plants and animals that died millions of years ago. We call them **fossil fuels**. People burn fossil fuels to release energy to make vehicles run or to make electricity. Burning fossil fuels produces more carbon dioxide.

People drill out fossil fuels from underground. They use these carbon compounds to power machines such as cars.

How Do We Make Compounds?

Some **compounds** are not found naturally. They are made by people from **elements** or compounds found on Earth. Two examples are glass and plastic.

Glass

People usually make glass by heating together sand, soda, and limestone. These commonly found compounds contain the elements that combine to form glass. Sand contains silicon, soda contains sodium, and limestone contains calcium. Heating makes the elements **react** with oxygen from the air, forming glass.

Glass is **transparent** and waterproof. These **physical properties** make it ideal for windows, lightbulbs, drinking glasses, and windshields. However, glass has some less useful properties. It is brittle and smashes easily into sharp pieces. One **chemical property** of glass is that it does not easily react with other substances.

Glass is an ideal material for windshields. The glass is strengthened with clear layers of plastic.

Plastics

Look around your home and you will find lots of things made from plastic, from TVs to bowls. Plastics are made up of long chains of compounds. The compounds used in plastics usually come from oil.

Plastics have very different physical properties, depending on how they are made. Soft, flexible plastic bags and rigid detergent bottles are made of a plastic called polyethylene. The plastic can be made softer or harder, depending on how strongly its chain of compounds is linked together.

Did you know?
PVC

Polyvinyl chloride (PVC) is a tough plastic used to make things such as pipes, window frames, and shoe soles. To make PVC, first, oil is heated to obtain a compound called ethylene. Then, ethylene is heated with chlorine and oxygen **gases** to produce a **chemical reaction** that makes vinyl chloride. Finally, another chemical reaction is used to stick vinyl chloride **molecules** together to form PVC chains.

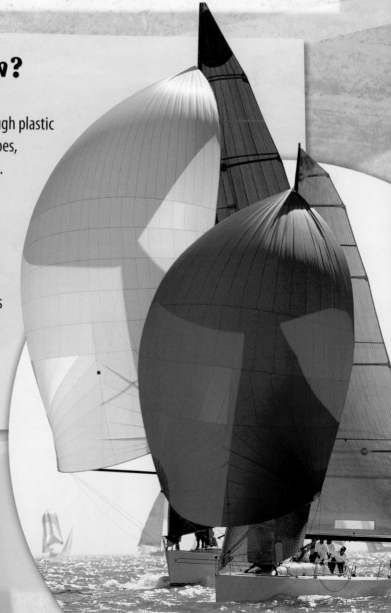

The tough, light, flexible material used in these sails was made from plastic strands.

Demonstration
Make slimy plastic

This demonstrates how a chemical reaction between two compounds can make a type of plastic. You should ask an adult to help you with this experiment.

You will need:
- white liquid glue
- Borax powder, which is often found near laundry detergent in stores
- food coloring of your choice
- two large glass bowls
- a measuring cup and teaspoon

Procedure:
1. In one bowl, mix two cups of glue, one and a half cups of warm water, and five drops of food coloring.
2. In the other bowl, mix four teaspoons of Borax and one and a third cups of warm water.
3. Pour the glue mixture into the Borax mixture and watch a cloud of rubbery slime form. This is the slimy plastic. Lift it out of the liquid, press it together, and play!

Warning:
- Your slime is safe to handle but NOT to eat, so wash your hands carefully after the demonstration.
- Colored slime could stain or stick to your clothes, so be careful!

PERIODIC TABLE

The **periodic table** was first put together in the 1860s by a scientist named Dmitry Mendeleyev. The **elements** are arranged in rows called periods, based on their properties and the size of their **atoms**.

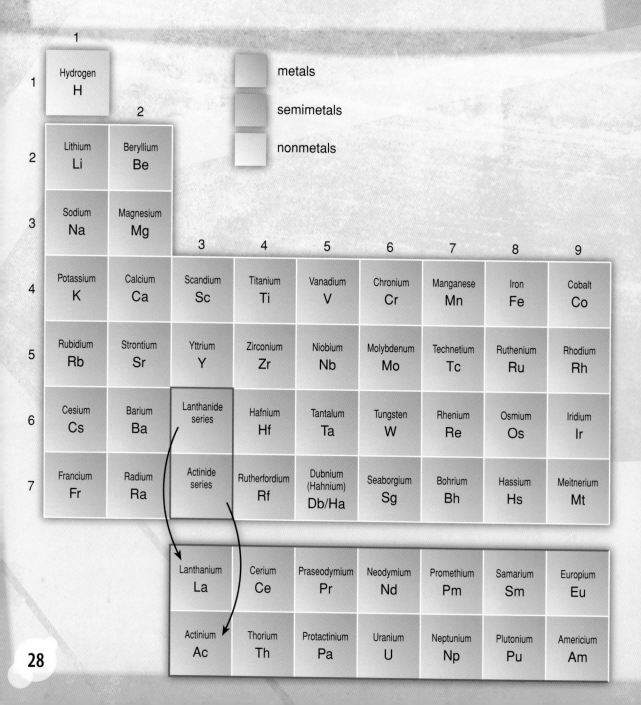

metals

semimetals

nonmetals

1		2		3	4	5	6	7	8	9
1 Hydrogen H										
2 Lithium Li	Beryllium Be									
3 Sodium Na	Magnesium Mg									
4 Potassium K	Calcium Ca	Scandium Sc	Titanium Ti	Vanadium V	Chronium Cr	Manganese Mn	Iron Fe	Cobalt Co
5 Rubidium Rb	Strontium Sr	Yttrium Y	Zirconium Zr	Niobium Nb	Molybdenum Mo	Technetium Tc	Ruthenium Ru	Rhodium Rh
6 Cesium Cs	Barium Ba	Lanthanide series	Hafnium Hf	Tantalum Ta	Tungsten W	Rhenium Re	Osmium Os	Iridium Ir
7 Francium Fr	Radium Ra	Actinide series	Rutherfordium Rf	Dubnium (Hahnium) Db/Ha	Seaborgium Sg	Bohrium Bh	Hassium Hs	Meitnerium Mt

Lanthanium La	Cerium Ce	Praseodymium Pr	Neodymium Nd	Promethium Pm	Samarium Sm	Europium Eu
Actinium Ac	Thorium Th	Protactinium Pa	Uranium U	Neptunium Np	Plutonium Pu	Americium Am

28

Below is a very simple version of the periodic table. It shows just the elements mentioned in this book, with their **chemical symbols**. The **metals**, **nonmetals**, and **semimetals** are shown in different-colored blocks. You can see that hydrogen is positioned a long way from other nonmetals. This is because it has **chemical properties** that are more like metals such as sodium than nonmetals such as helium.

			13	14	15	16	17	18
								Helium He
			Boron B	Carbon C	Nitrogen N	Oxygen O	Fluorine F	Neon Ne
			Aluminum Al	Silicon Si	Phosphorus P	Sulfur S	Chlorine Cl	Argon Ar
10	11	12						
Nickel Ni	Copper Cu	Zinc Zn	Gallium Ga	Germanium Ge	Arsenic As	Selenium Se	Bromine Br	Krypton Kr
Palladium Pd	Silver Ag	Cadmium Cd	Indium In	Tin Sn	Antimony Sb	Tellurium Te	Iodine I	Xenon Xe
Platinum Pt	Gold Au	Mercury Hg	Thallium Tl	Lead Pb	Bismuth Bi	Polonium Po	Astatine At	Radon Rn
Darmstadtium Ds	Roentgenium Rg				Ununpentium Uup			

Gadolinium Gd	Terbium Tb	Dysprosium Dy	Holmium Ho	Erbium Er	Thulium Tm	Ytterbium Yb	Lutetium Lu
Curium Cm	Berkelium Bk	Californium Cf	Einsteinium Es	Fermium Fm	Mendelevium Md	Nobelium No	Lawrencium Lr

Glossary

atom one of the tiny particles that make up matter

bond force caused by electrons pulling different atoms or molecules together

chemical property describes how a substance behaves when combined with other substances

chemical reaction when substances combine to form a new substance with different chemical properties

chemical symbol letter or letters, often with numbers, used to represent an element or compound

compound substance formed from two or more substances that has different chemical properties than either

conduct move electricity through a substance

conductor any material that heat or electricity can move through

dissolve mix completely into another substance

electricity force caused by movement of electrons through a conductor

electron tiny part of an atom moving around the nucleus

element substance containing one type of atom

fossil fuel natural fuel such as oil, gas, or coal, formed from the remains of living things trapped between layers of rock millions of years ago

gas state of matter in which atoms or molecules are furthest apart

liquid state of matter in which atoms or molecules are weakly held together with a definite volume but variable shape

magnetism force that causes some metals to move together or apart

melt change from solid to liquid state

metal element such as iron. Metals have similar properties, such as a high melting point.

molecule two or more atoms joined together

nonmetal one of two main groups of elements. Nonmetals are generally poor conductors, not shiny, and melt at low temperatures.

ore mineral that contains metal

particle very small piece of material

periodic table chart showing all elements arranged by their properties

physical property characteristic of a substance, such as its state or hardness

react undergo a chemical reaction

reversible change that can go backward or forward

rust reddish, crumbly powder formed when iron reacts with oxygen

semimetal one of a group of elements with properties partly like metals and partly like nonmetals

solid state of matter in which atoms or molecules are packed tightly together in a definite shape

state form of matter—solid, liquid, or gas

transparent clear, allowing light to pass through

Further Resources

Books

Baldwin, Carol. *Mixtures, Compounds, and Solutions* (*Freestyle Express: Material Matters* series). Chicago: Raintree, 2006.

Llewellyn, Claire. *Material World* series. New York: Franklin Watts, 2002.

Oxlade, Chris. *Elements and Compounds* (*Chemicals in Action* series). Chicago: Heinemann Library, 2002.

Websites

Find out more about elements and compounds at:
http://www.chem4kids.com/files/elem_intro.html

To learn more about the elements, click on the symbols in the periodic table at:
http://www.chemicalelements.com/

Index